MAIDEN
MOTHER
CRONE

Amba Elieff

With Illustrations by
Gabrielle Elizabeth Scarlett

Copyright © 2022 Amba Elieff (@amba.elieff)
Illustrations Copyright © 2022 Gabrielle Elizabeth
Scarlett (@thegabriellescarlett)

If you are inspired to post images of the pages of this text on social media, please tag @amba.elieff. I would love to witness you on your journey.

All rights reserved.
ISBN: 9798835235520

POETRY OF LIFE'S CHANGES

This is my first collection of poetry. It is a combination of poems that reach back into my childhood and some that were written a month ago. All the phases of my life (maiden, mother, and crone) are touched on here. I have shared some of these poems on social media. I am always amazed when people recognize themselves in the poems. I always wrote for me to get clarity and to heal and to get rid of baggage. But now that that I am older I realize that I also write to share so others will know that they aren't alone. We all struggle and celebrate and survive. Some of us just put all that into words.

I am a plain poet
my prose is not full of literary devices
flowery words
it is written
to tell stories
some last a minute
some last a lifetime
in a short form
accessible
so I can share my life
with you
and touch you
and for a moment we are together

- amba elieff

CONTENTS

Acknowledgments i

Maiden 1
Mother 41
Crone 91
Prompt Me 168

ACKNOWLEDGMENTS

Here are the thank yous.

To P.K. Smith who was my English teacher in high school. She was the first person who told me I would be a writer one day.

To Dr. Jeff Sommers who was one of my professors and my adviser in college. He told me my freshman year that I wrote well enough to become a writer if I kept writing.

To my husband who always believes in me and supports me no matter what.

To my daughter who put in many hours doing layout and graphics and editing and reading and telling me I was a badass when I didn't feel like one.

Maiden, Mother, Crone

To Sergio Gonzalez, I believe that sometimes there are humans that are angels that visit us, messengers. Sergio was one of those. Right before I was laid off and I completely redefined my world. I worked with him. He was a young guy who was fresh out of college. We had one of those strange undefinable connections. At a holiday gift exchange where we drew numbers and got our gift, I got the one from him. He told me that he bought it hoping I would be the one to get it. It was a trigger point massage tool and an old book of poetry by Ella Wheeler Wilcox, Poems of Passion from 1883. I genuinely believe that he was showing me my future. He is one of the angels that drop feathers letting me know he is watching.

And thank you to you for choosing to read my poetry. I hope you find something that touches you, makes you laugh, and lets you know that you are not alone.

Maiden, Mother, Crone

MAIDEN

Maiden, Mother, Crone

Maiden, Mother, Crone

Today I give myself the grace
to start something
to not do it perfectly
to have it be messy
to look foolish
to be wrong
and to glow with the satisfaction
that I started

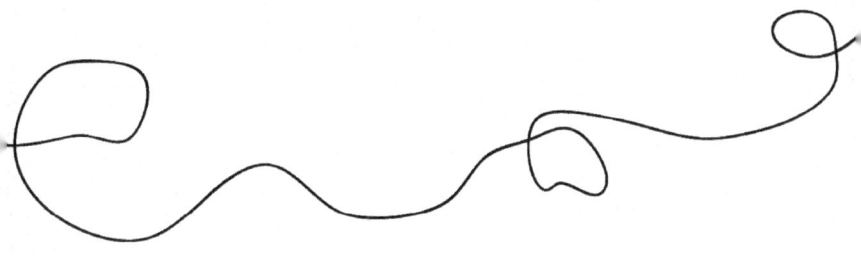

- amba elieff

Maiden, Mother, Crone

I bundle up in my grape down coat, hat, and wool mittens
I tip toe to the hammock trying not to disturb the snow
I lay down, face full to the sky, white below - white above
I close my eyes and feel the flakes turn to cold tears on my warm cheeks
I hum a few mantras feeling the vibration through my body
    as the flakes tap a tune on my down coat
Sending good healing energy to the earth
Then I hear the birds join my hum
I am silent
They continue singing far off songs and promises of spring
Enveloped in the beauty of it all I am humbled
My grape coat turns white
Then the crash of the neighbor yelling at her dogs
I go inside, but part of me is still floating there
In that space, white below - white above

- amba elieff

Maiden, Mother, Crone

The snow is clean, smooth, and rounded as a perfectly
    iced wedding cake
The angels not yet risen by small child bodies
The beauty not yet marred by paw prints and yellow
    snow
So flawless and pure I don't yet want to touch it
with the crunch of my footsteps
or the bouncing of the dogs
So I let the snow sleep a little longer

- amba elieff

Deep sigh of contentment this morning
The complete silence of a pure white blanket of snow,
come to cover us all in the night
Cleansing and purifying all the world of its
filth, shame, noise so the earth can awaken again in spring
    with the birth
of flowers and sunshine rays that make the eyes see
    rainbows
I give thanks

- amba elieff

Maiden, Mother, Crone

I was born in a field somewhere, a cabbage patch, in the woods under a tree
That is what my mind has given me
It is a gift
I know I was not planned
I was not wanted
I was not an easy birth
I was accepted as one might accept the weather
Not exactly what you wanted but you can't change it
You live with it
And I was raised
And from the outside things looked as they should
And inside I was alone
I was ignored in conversations
My opinions did not exist
No one was interested in me
So I was born in the woods under a tree
The flowers and animals were my friends
I took care of them
We understood each other
There was love and peace under the trees
One day when I am old and tired
I will return there and curl up under the trees
The animals and flowers will visit me one more time
And I will return to the place where I was born

- amba elieff

Maiden, Mother, Crone

A poem can be a story
a memory
a feeling
a place
a catharsis
It can be loud
or quiet
It can be a place to hide
or a place to bare everything
A place where you are raw and naked
in front of everyone
Baring your soul
In the hopes you might heal

- amba elieff

Maiden, Mother, Crone

The trestle rises high up into the air
old and forgotten
I walk on top where the grass is growing over the tracks
the earth is solid here
Then temptation and fate, a simple dare
I climb down to walk across again
this time from the latticework of wood that holds the tracks above
The board beneath my feet is the width of my foot
I can't look down
Exhilarating
what if I fall
I hear my heart beat
I am half way out going forward is the same as going back
I feel the wind
I reach out to steady myself
I am moving painfully slow
why am I doing this
I can feel my heart beat faster
I am free of everything here on the trestle
for a moment
Then I take the last step back to solid earth
Trapped again by its firm predictability

- amba elieff

Maiden, Mother, Crone

Flowers
Most guys give flowers
They are standard
They are colorful and pretty
And they die
The moment that they are cut to give to you
They begin a slow death
And you watch it
And then you throw them away
A bouquet of death
Give me plants
Something I can nurture, love
That as long as it is with me I think of you
Flowers that visit me every year
Until the day I die

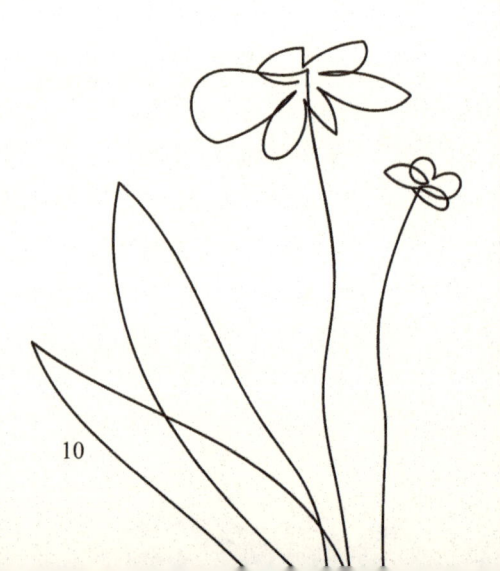

- amba elieff

Maiden, Mother, Crone

In the depths of the refrigerator,
lies the stuff I prefer to let
rot and mold –
Onions aged their sickeningly, sweet stench
permeating the air.
Oysters all cold, clammy, slimy,
jelling in their muck.
Swiss cheese with its rubbery, sourness
flaking green around the brittle edges.
But here's what I've been looking for –
the curling iron, on the top shelf...

- amba elieff

Maiden, Mother, Crone

He sat beside me
and took my hand
Quiet
Patient
No expectations
No questions
No conversation
I looked at him
and I asked
why
He smiled
I'm here to believe in you
until you can

- amba elieff

I can't sleep alone in our bed
when you are gone
your empty spot is too cold
Your body not there to protect me
make me feel safe
offer it's warmth
There is too much space
So I retreat to the couch
and try to find some rest
there

- amba elieff

Maiden, Mother, Crone

Please let me recognize the right one
not the perfect one
the one that is imperfect
who will hold my heart gentle and safe
and touch my soul
like butterfly wings
who will send in fireflies
dancing magic light in the air
who will kiss the top of my head
and tuck me into his shoulder
so I fall asleep to the sound of his heartbeat
let me know the right one

- amba elieff

Maiden, Mother, Crone

When he is away
the silence descends
quiet
my thoughts remain in my head
nowhere to go
the minutia of daily existence
no longer shared
no one to hear
no one to tell
I forget how to talk
how to share myself
silence prolonged
til I can find my voice
days after you return
and the minutia that was important is gone

- amba elieff

Maiden, Mother, Crone

Everything about me
each moment
feeling
thought
trapped in my body
becomes real
in poetry
when I put words on the page
I am no longer a quiet mouse
I have a voice
and I am alive
and I matter
All of me that no one knew existed
released into the world

- amba elieff

Maiden, Mother, Crone

Child of the cold war
nuclear bombs dropped on Japan
a history lesson
a mushroom cloud
an imagination
of being vaporized
does it hurt
of being deformed
what would I look like
of being changed in ways
my brain could not yet
comprehend
just like the inability
to comprehend
the kind of hate
that would require such a bomb
that holds us hostage
in a cold war

- amba elieff

Maiden, Mother, Crone

I would like to just be sick
just for a day
to take time to rest
let my body be
read
sleep
stare
at nothing
no responsibility
no demands
or expectations
my energy all my own
tucked around me
til my weary soul
feels rested and well

- amba elieff

My mind fills up
thoughts
words
images
and it empties
on a page
through a pen
it is a pulse
it is like breathing
it is my life

- amba elieff

Maiden, Mother, Crone

Homesick is the moment
when you realize
that you can't go home
until that moment it is an adventure
it can be a day
a weekend
a month
or years
that adventure
suddenly ends
overwhelmed with the desire to go home
but you can't

- amba elieff

Maiden, Mother, Crone

Self-worth
I never feel important
Was not raised to feel I was valued
I accept that
it is part of me
and I silently beg
please make me important

- amba elieff

Maiden, Mother, Crone

I love
curling up
under old quilts

Maiden, Mother, Crone

closing my eyes
and listening
to their stories

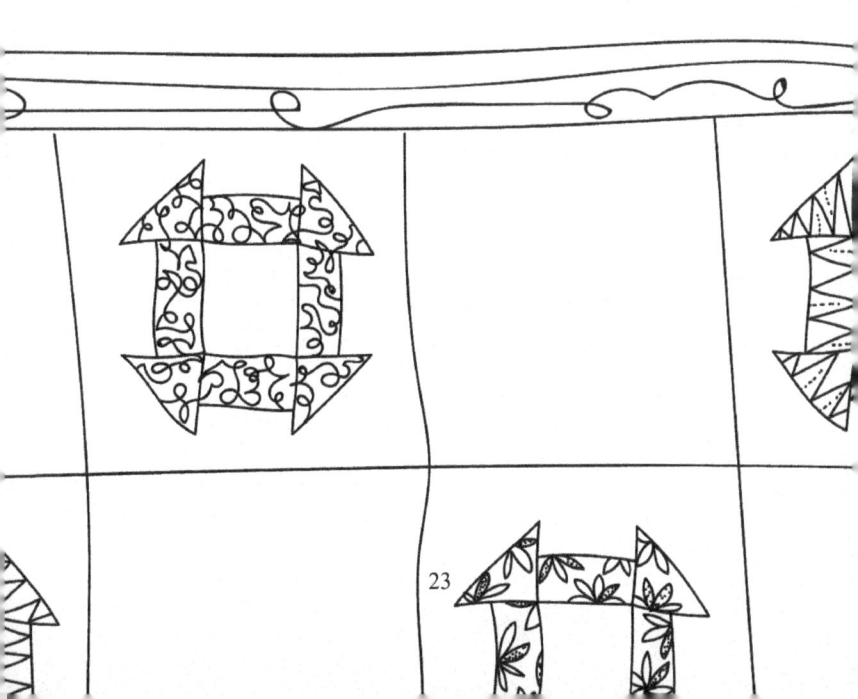

- *amba elieff*

Lied
I lied a lot
it was a survival skill
growing up
a way to try to
have a normal world
lie to be with friends
lie to go places
lie to go on a date
lie to simply do things
none of them wrong
none of them bad
just to be a normal teenager
required a lie
so it was never normal

- amba elieff

Maiden, Mother, Crone

Once you no longer
have to lie
to survive
and you live in the truth
you always wonder
if everyone else
is actually
telling the truth

- amba elieff

Maiden, Mother, Crone

Liar
I don't think so
not a label I would use
wasn't good at it
simple
trying to present a life
have a life
living with the constant
anxiety
of lies
which are secrets
held close inside
scared of being caught
in the story that you created
but no other place to go

- amba elieff

Maiden, Mother, Crone

Dad
Is a collection of atta girls
Is mowing the grass
Fertilizing the grass
Edging the yard
It must look perfect
Is sweeping up the last blades of cut grass from the sidewalk
Is raking up the last leaf in the yard and putting it in the bag

I am grown
I mow the grass mixed with weeds
I do not fertilize the grass
    I do not sweep the blades of grass from the sidewalks
There is wind for that
I do not rake the leaves
except for piles
for my children to jump in
crunching them on their way down

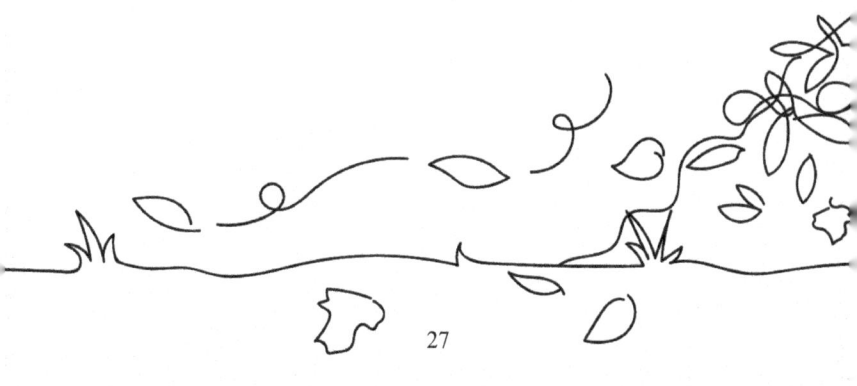

- amba elieff

Maiden, Mother, Crone

You may think of it as a search engine
For me Google is
The one I ask how long to boil an egg
How to make a favorite food I remember as a child
How to get that spot out of my favorite shirt
How to make the gravy
How to braid their hair
Google and my mother are both just a cell phone away
But I can't ask my mother
Google is less of a stranger
The only thing
Google can't answer is
How can I ask my mother how long to boil an egg...

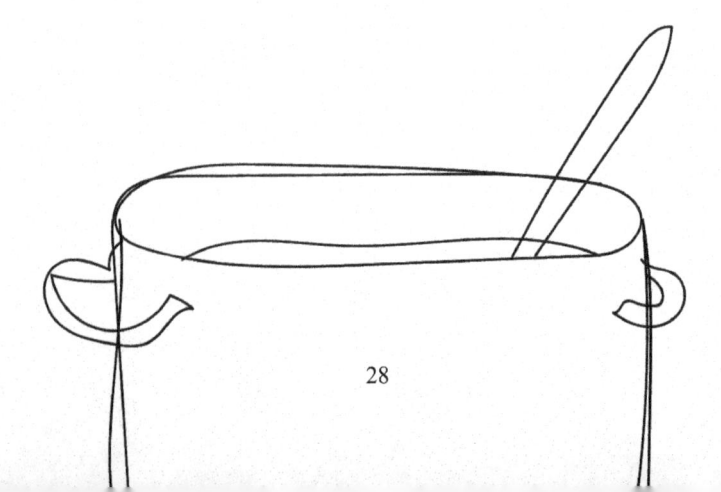

- amba elieff

Maiden, Mother, Crone

All of my paths and roads are twisty
Full of ups and downs
Hills and valleys
There is no direct path to get to the place I am heading toward
There is sunshine leading sometimes and then there are shadows
But I trust and I keep moving forward
Round the bends
Waiting expectantly to see what is just out of view
Somehow knowing it will be another curve
Excited for the view at the top of the hill
Pensive heading toward a valley
Another bend
Darkness
But that is okay
because somewhere up ahead
there will be more sunshine leading the way
I just need to keep moving forward...

- amba elieff

I feel out of place here
Never like I belong
Like an ice cube in the oven
Like a swimsuit in the arctic
Like skis in the desert
Like a tree in the ocean
Like a turtle flying in the sky
Like the sunshine if it were underground
How do I make me belong
How can I feel right....

- amba elieff

There was always a crescent moon
He was the light and I was the dark shadow he carried
He was the laughter and I was the silence he buoyed
Until one day, I found a waterfall
I was the laughter crashing over the rocks carrying him
    with me
I was the reflection of the sun that sparkled and warmed
    us
And for a moment, it was me who made us one

- amba elieff

Maiden, Mother, Crone

How many Benadryl
to never wake up?
one makes me sleepy
no place to find information
No internet
No how-to in a library
I will pick seven
and go to bed
and hope I just sleep
forever

- amba elieff

Maiden, Mother, Crone

The world was full
of tunnels
with no way out
dark
endless
no escape
only dreams of escape
day dreams I could control
life had no control
just tunnels
and questions
why am i here?

- amba elieff

Maiden, Mother, Crone

They are searching
for someone
to take responsibility of me
cause I am a girl
so they will no longer
be on the hook

- amba elieff

Maiden, Mother, Crone

The house
where I grew up
was made of eggshells
sound
movement
thoughts
feelings
jarred the structure
move quietly
speak quiet voice
a sudden emotion
might bring the entire house
down

- amba elieff

Maiden, Mother, Crone

I know they thought
they did right by me
the best they could
with what they had
to work with
but I wouldn't mold
couldn't bend
easier to ignore
til they couldn't
be quiet
and the words
stabbing
scarring
still echoing
inside my mind
still hurt
after all this time

- amba elieff

Maiden, Mother, Crone

No one knew
No one suspected
Extra key on her keychain
days of sneaking out boxes
Everything planned
A friend showed up
Normal day
F150
They emptied her room
10X12
bed
dressers
clothes
books
her mother watched on
her father was at work
In a handful of hours
She had flown the coop
as she left
a few tears from her mother
and
"you are just like your aunt..."
it was not a compliment
and I was gone...

- amba elieff

Maiden, Mother, Crone

We are humans
I was small
and grew
in a shared space
One third of my life
you rubbed off on me
imbedded beliefs on me
a view of the world
sharing nothing but space
and what you could imprint on me
a child
no real ties
connections
I grew
and left
and we are humans
no longer sharing space

- amba elieff

Maiden, Mother, Crone

He lives in a box
created by time
created by habits
created by family
beliefs
perceptions
attitudes
never changing
never learning
how to be
tender
warm
no daddy's little girl
so he stays in the box
and I look
from outside
without a way
to be in his box

- amba elieff

Maiden, Mother, Crone

MOTHER

Maiden, Mother, Crone

Maiden, Mother, Crone

Today the phone rang
it started the avalanche
of things to do
I deleted the files
I wasn't to touch, but didn't know
that went out to the place where lost socks and mittens go
never to be found again
I felt bad, rotten, sorry, helpless
Then I look over and see her
she smiles
she found her toes today...

- amba elieff

Maiden, Mother, Crone

I am at home all day
chasing kids
wiping mouths sticky with chocolate
making beds
picking up toys
creating a path to the kitchen and bathroom
changing diapers
typing on my computer
listening to conference calls
answering emails
cooking lunch
washing clothes with spots like a rainbow
smooshed carrots, squished peas, more chocolate
reading stories
changing diapers
pushing swings
washing dishes
answering why and how come
so tell me where are the bon-bons

- amba elieff

Maiden, Mother, Crone

He left me today
the one who gave me hopes and dreams
promised me companionship and love
has left me with an empty bed

So, I stand in front of the fridge
as the moon watches outside
and I wonder
are there less calories
if I just eat the chocolate chip cookie dough raw

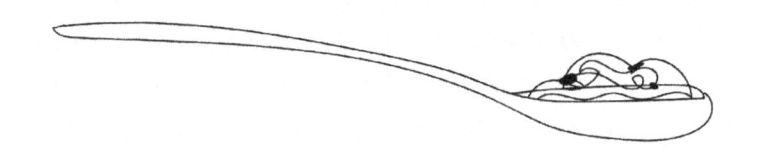

- amba elieff

Maiden, Mother, Crone

Where are my socks?
where are my shoes?
my sunglasses, my keys, the sun, the moon –
would you, could you help me please
you see I have the man's disease

Where is the toilet paper?
where is the soap?
I stare in the closet, it isn't a joke
would you, could you help me please
you see I have the man's disease

Where is the paper?
where is the mail?
I look on the desk, I rummage the pail
would you, could you help me please
you see I have the man's disease

The man's disease, the man's disease
frustrating, aggravating, blinding disease
I look, I stare, it's never there
you see I have the man's disease

- amba elieff

Maiden, Mother, Crone

I remember joy
the feel of it light in my body
the wonder in my face
eyes wide with amazement
A floaty feeling
The scent of everything undiscovered
and clean and pure
The light that radiated from the deepest recesses of my body
bouncing off everything
Infusing everything with my light
my wonder
I want to feel that again
But it feels so lost
so buried
joy and its light are lost – right now

- amba elieff

Maiden, Mother, Crone

She sits there and looks at me
eyes wide and innocent
"Why do Daddys leave?"
and what do I say
because they are unhappy
because they need their space
because they need to think
because they get confused
because...
Someone please tell Me,
why do daddies leave

- amba elieff

Maiden, Mother, Crone

Maiden, Mother, Crone

I have awakened to the sounds of buzzers
like bees in my ear
I have been jarred from slumberland
by music, birds singing, and
children playing in the street
But the sweetest alarm I will ever hear
is the tiny voice hollering
"Mommy, I have to potty!"
at 6:00 in the morning

- amba elieff

Maiden, Mother, Crone

I wanted you to potty, in your potty
No more diapers –
I got you to potty, in your potty
but sometimes like a fountain, over the edge it goes
and sometimes you try to watch and over the edge it goes
I wipe up the little puddle and splash, a wet spot on the
    floor
again and again and again and again
but
I got you to potty, in your potty
And all of it in the potty
finally diapers are no more

- amba elieff

Maiden, Mother, Crone

I look at the percentages that rule my life
10% is always top honors at school
20% is the promises that were kept
30% is the number of hot dinners on the table
40% is the deadlines that are made
50% is always a really, good sale
60% is the percentage of divorce
where I never thought I would be

- amba elieff

Maiden, Mother, Crone

When he is gone
I will leave the twist tie off the bread
leave the leftovers on the stove til bedtime
put flowered wallpaper in the bedroom
sit outside and howl at the moon

When he is gone
I will create my IRA
squirrel money away for a rainy day
pick my expenses
sit outside and howl at the moon

When he is gone
I will let the kids make noise
crawl in bed with me after the bad dream
serve macaroni and chicken nuggets at every meal
sit outside and howl at the moon
while the children catch lightning bugs

And the bugs will light our way
and the stars will give us hope
and our noise will tell us we are not alone

- amba elieff

Maiden, Mother, Crone

I asked my husband
for Halloween, please
dress up as a family man.

Wear your polo shirt and sneakers
kiss me good-bye
hold the girls' hands
protect them from the monsters and ghouls
laugh at their silly songs
tease them a little, so they know they are loved
walk tirelessly from house to house
bring our girl's back home safe to me
so we can tuck them in bed
and chase away all their fears
then hold me tight all through the night
and for a moment I might imagine
that you are a real family man
and the family man is home to stay

- amba elieff

Maiden, Mother, Crone

Grandparent's prayer
Now, I lay me down to sleep
Grandchildren tucked in and fast asleep
I pray to God before he's done
To bring their parents' home one by one
I am retired
I've raised my own
The golf course and bingo hall should be my home

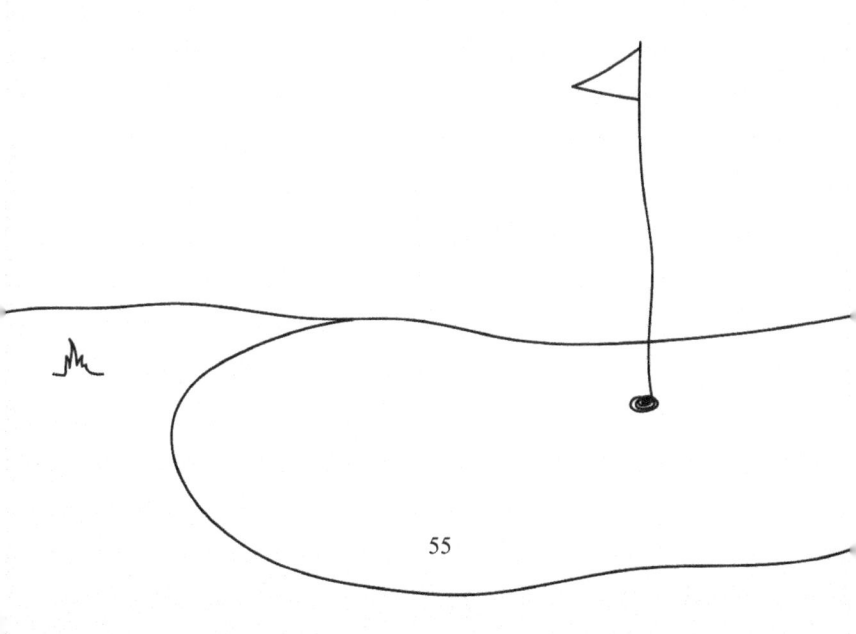

- amba elieff

Maiden, Mother, Crone

It is quiet tonight
a sleeping child is missing
the quiet is unnerving
she is safe and sound
tucked in at Grandma's
but I listen
for the heartbeat that
is missing in my house
for the night

- amba elieff

Maiden, Mother, Crone

I am having a tea party with Miss Brie
candy and chocolate,
BBQ chips and cheese,
chocolate chip cookies and Kool-Aid,
pass the ice cream please
and I sit and wonder why
they decided
to enrich flour instead of chocolate

- amba elieff

Maiden, Mother, Crone

We sit and stare at each other
I am the liberated female
which gives me the right
to cook dinner
to clean the house
to mow the yard
to raise the children
to paint the basement
to plant the flowers
to wash the dishes
to work and earn a living
to fix the broken things
His eyes are sad
Now, he is simply redundant

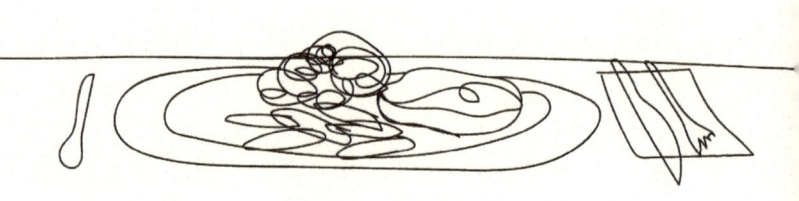

- amba elieff

Maiden, Mother, Crone

I try to reconcile my face
It is unremarkable
Lived with it my entire life
I am not fond of it
We tolerate each other my face and I
Eyebrows that grow together, perpetually plucking
Brown eyes deep dark pits
my mother wanted them to be blue
High cheekbones now slightly gaunt with age
A smile always too toothy and too big
I look at these pieces that I have taken care of
Trying to find something beautiful about them
When I look and see that same eyebrow on my youngest
who does have blue eyes
And I see the expressive brown eyes in my oldest
And they both have the high cheekbones that on them are
    elegant
And both of their smiles are perfect even when they smile
    like me
And I realize I have found something beautiful in my
    face...my daughters

- amba elieff

Maiden, Mother, Crone

I keep you in a box in the basement
It is a simple plastic tote
Something impervious to water and safe
The contents regularly change
There was the beginning of the box
Filled with handprint turkeys, crooked heart valentines,
the first spelling test, carefully drawn letters, your name printed
Then you got older and I didn't worry about losing you quite so young
cause you never know
the world is a chaotic place and things happen
and one day someone you hold dear is gone
So the box became filled with paintings, pottery, music, essays
pictures of my teenage girl, loose crystals and beads and pressed flowers
And the sigh of relief that you were still safe
And then you went away to college
Again the box changed
I was able to give thanks I had you almost 19 years now
And the box filled with notes, more professional paintings and pictures,
dissertations, achievements

Maiden, Mother, Crone

And you became successful and all I could have hoped
And now you are over an ocean
The pottery is strewn about my house
I touch it – and think of touching you
And I have many boxes of all the things that you couldn't take
And from your cast off books and clothes I have sprinkled my shelves and closets with pieces of you
And in each of them I see you
And you are not so far away

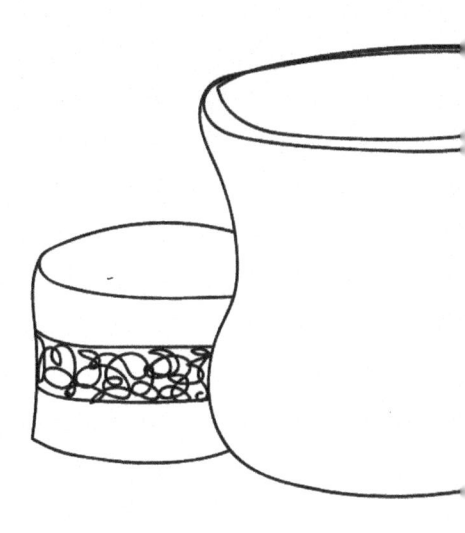

- amba elieff

Maiden, Mother, Crone

There is more to me than this
than waking up to do all the dishes
cleaning the house
paying the bills
and trading the work of my hands, arms, back, and legs
for just enough to just cover the bills
stopping the dreams
there is no money for dreams
no vacations
no travel
only work
and worrying about money
and bills
and healthcare
Anything that is more
got shoved under the reality of life
and the dishes, and the bills, and the work

- amba elieff

Maiden, Mother, Crone

I arrived in the middle of the story
You were no longer a child
But not yet grown
That place in the middle
And the house was not my house
The silverware was already in its drawer
With the spoons mixed big and little
And there were no meals at a table
And everything was everywhere
And I moved some things
Found better homes for dish towels
Organized cupboards
Put up a family calendar
Added my traditions with the house's
Lived with meals in the living room
And years from the middle
I made dinner and you set the table
And you made me a gift for Solstice
You claimed me as a part of you...

- amba elieff

Maiden, Mother, Crone

I tried
and I tried
and I waited
and I hoped
and I tried again
til after so much time
the letters got scrambled
in my mouth and my head
and I just got tired
so tired
there were no tries left
and I waited
and I hoped
too tired to do anything else
the only place left to go
is to be done
which is the end
please don't make me be done

- amba elieff

Maiden, Mother, Crone

What will you remember of me
I wonder
feathers
that they are whispers
of angels that visit
saltines and coke for
upset tummies
or sometimes seven-up
Once you put anything
on the internet it lives forever
be careful what you post
Always do your best
that is good enough
If you feel bored enjoy it
those moments don't come that often
Knowledge is power
read everything
never stop learning
Appreciate everything the good and the bad
because everything happens for a reason
we just might not be able to see it
Look at the flowers
and all the world that lives on them
know that you share that world with everything that is
You are equal to each tree, animal, bug and the dirt
below your feet
Tread lightly
and that feather
it is me
Love Mom

- amba elieff

Maiden, Mother, Crone

Each time I question
me
my worth
my existence
my purpose
the jar of feathers
reminds me how often
your angel blessings
have watched over me
each one a blessing from you
reminding me
I am valuable
I am loved
my life does have meaning
And you are watching

- amba elieff

Maiden, Mother, Crone

My daughter saw me
naked and raw
and vulnerable
I let her read my words
these were scars
she had never seen
the depth of the wounds
the jagged edges
the brutal reality
of the daily demons
that rule my world

- amba elieff

Maiden, Mother, Crone

Sometimes I try to remember what 10 looked like
Flat chested
Short hair
Bright Eyes
At least I hope they were bright for a little while

I remember frustration as old men still called her young man
Thanks for holding the door young man
Her favorite color was blue
She would get angry when people would mistake her for a boy
I bought her a pink hat
It helped

I have photos in albums on a shelf
I have photos on my computer organized in files
By year
By event

I could look at them
But I am scared

Scared that I will see in her eyes
What I missed
When she was 10

Maiden, Mother, Crone

Scared that I will see the picture that shows the change
The moment that secrets ruled her world
   and she aged

The disillusion
The confusion
The sadness

Sometimes I try to remember what 10 looked like
I wish I could make it look different

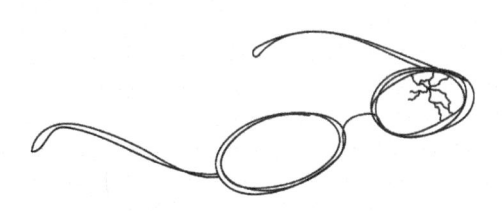

- amba elieff

Maiden, Mother, Crone

Cereal and Chocolate both start with C
We eat lots of it
Cereal and Chocolate
This is a house of girls
Cereal is an easy meal
I have boxes
And boxes
And boxes

We are company independent
General foods, Quaker, Kellogg
There is Krave
Both double chocolate and just chocolate
There is Special K
The kind with the chocolate chunks
There are Cheerios
Chocolate, Dulce de leche, banana and just plain ole cheerios

Then there are some fruits
Captain Crunch with crunch berries
The girls find it strange that I buy this
Remarkably it has none of the bad stuff
Like partially hydrogenated soybean oil or high fructose corn syrup
It is probably made the same way it was when I was a child

Maiden, Mother, Crone

That is a requirement for the cereal in the house that it
    not have these evil things
And that it does have fruit or chocolate
Especially chocolate

There is Special K with the red berries
The red berries are strawberries
That is fruit
If you pour it in a bowl with the Chocolate chunk Special
    K
You get strawberries with chocolate
Yummy

There is some just plain cereal like the plain ole cheerios
There are Wheeties
But they are for putting on casseroles to make crunch
And mostly for putting with ice cream
To make fried ice cream
Which does include chocolate
Which we always need

- amba elieff

Maiden, Mother, Crone

Maiden, Mother, Crone

I walk barefoot through my kitchen
crumbs stick to my toes
Then my heel finds the sticky spot
where the juice dripped
There is a collection of handprints
on the refrigerator
    Tiny fingerprints
I ponder the one that has tinges of green
My Mom's house always seemed so clean
No dirty fingers to make fingerprints
No dripped juice left sticky on a floor
I hope my daughters remember
I loved their fingerprints and sticky spots too

- amba elieff

Maiden, Mother, Crone

My Mother-in-law
    Once a week I clean the floors
I know yours have always been spotless
Twice a week I make the beds
I know yours are done early in the morn
Three times a week I throw together a good dinner
leftovers and hotdogs often suffice
I know you cook a good meal fresh every night, always have
My laundry and ironing pile up til I have to
Yours was always done and tucked away
But everyday I clean little fingers and toes,
read stories, and play peek-a-boo
I fix little meals with crusts cut off and carrots hidden beneath noodles
I make pillow houses and tents, kiss boo-boos
I holler don't pick your nose, stand up on the chair, pull your sister's hair
Everyday I am a Mom

- amba elieff

Maiden, Mother, Crone

Your little arms would creep around my neck
as I tucked you into bed
"Stay with me Mommy" you always said
One more hug and kiss as I tucked you into bed
"Stay with me Mommy" you always said
I would start to walk out the door and say good-night
You called for one more hug tonight
Your little arms would hug so tight
"Stay with me Mommy" you always said
Then we would both hear the little cry from the living
　room
You'd pause and pull away
"Go take care of her Mommy, no stay with me Mommy,
　she needs you Mommy"
My first baby's tucked in bed

- amba elieff

Maiden, Mother, Crone

Did too
Did not
Did too
Did not
Did to
Did not
Did to
Did not
Did to
Did not
Did what
Don't know

- amba elieff

Maiden, Mother, Crone

Sleeping like a parent
I wake up
it is 3:00 AM
full awake I trudge
off to the bathroom
swollen belly leads the way

I wake up
it is 3:00 AM
full awake I trudge
off to the nursery
baby's cries lead the way

I wake up
at 3:00 AM
full awake I trudge
off to the baby's room
cries from a toddler's nightmare
leads the way

I wake up
at 3:00 AM
full awake I trudge
off to check the rooms
child by child

I never sleep at 3:00 AM
I have teenagers now...

- amba elieff

Maiden, Mother, Crone

I am going to be decadent tonight
I will curl up in my bed
and roll over on my belly
I will lay there and stretch
my back towards the ceiling
I may drool onto the pillow
a little
You can't do that sleeping
on your back
I may sleep this way all night
on my belly
What a delightful way to celebrate
the birth of my baby

- amba elieff

Maiden, Mother, Crone

I stare at the ring on my finger
the ring of hope and promise
seven stones that I searched for meaning
rubies were friendship, the diamond was marriage
a twisted band for the blending of our happiness together
but the seven betrayed me
it was seven for sadness
rubies for commitment, the diamond for leaving
the twisted band that held them
the children who will be grieving

- amba elieff

Maiden, Mother, Crone

There is nothing extraordinary about my day
I toast a waffle and pour the milk
I empty the potty and change a diaper
I wash a little body, fingers, and toes...
Pease porridge and little piggy
The cow jumped over the moon
Barney and kool-aid, fish sticks and fries
I read the stories, kiss the boo-boos,
and tuck them in
I hear the laughter and squeals of delight
I see the first steps and the toothless smile
I am a Mommy, staying at home
How Extraordinary...

- amba elieff

Maiden, Mother, Crone

I clean the toilet that we both use
I change the bed that we both sleep in
I cook the dinner that we both eat
and wash the dishes that we both dirty
Day after day without a thought...
then
I reach the point
I don't know if it is the 45th time I change the bed
or the
103rd time I clean the toilet
wipe up the hair out of the tub
or the
307th time I return his shoes to his room
but
I reach the point when I don't want to anymore
the scary point when I wish he would leave
the tired point when I want him to be me

- amba elieff

Maiden, Mother, Crone

You couldn't have known
No one said anything
told
that is why it is called
a secret
comforting
No
real
Yes
But I still ask
could I have known

- amba elieff

Maiden, Mother, Crone

Children nurtured
raised
to leave the nest
fly and soar
become amazing beings
grow and thrive
I was not nurtured
to fly and soar
I simply
flew the coop
feeling my way
stumbling along

- amba elieff

Maiden, Mother, Crone

December
Early morning
I call the detectives
I set the time
10:15
control call
detectives record a call
a confession
early morning
10:00
cutting onions
tears and snotty nose
dicing, mincing
detectives arrive
confused
at my culinary activities
I snuff snot
Ready - I'm making chili
he will talk this time
I call
recorder ready
ringing
ringing
record button pressed
hello
tears and snot
Hi
awkward
and I stutter
I just need to know the truth
silence
I won't tell anyone
I promise

Maiden, Mother, Crone

and finally
he talks
tears on my cheeks
confession
and the detective
looking at me
realizing
I wasn't making chili

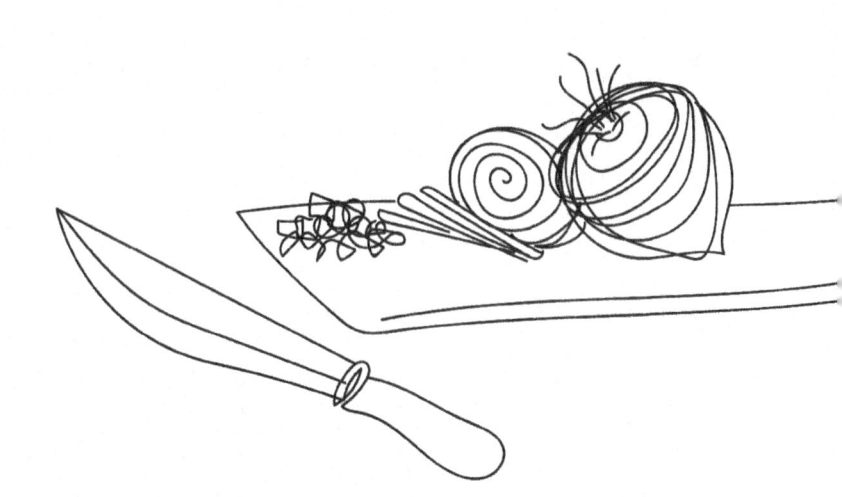

- amba elieff

Maiden, Mother, Crone

It played out
in the course of an evening
hours
the baby existed for mere hours
the period was late
a couple days
thought nothing of it
til it was several days
and the thought happened
I could be pregnant
shock
this wasn't supposed to happen
I had all my children
I was on birth control
careful
the mind begins to process
the thought
there could be a baby
all the changes in my life that would mean
my children's lives they were more than half grown
how would I manage
what would this new life look like
I called the father
to let him know the possibility
he...
and within the span of hours
I accepted I was going to have a baby
and I loved him or her unquestionable, unconditional
love
and a belief that it would be hard and it would be
wonderful
and I got home
cozy with the idea

Maiden, Mother, Crone

and I peed on the stick
and it was negative
I was simply late – no baby
and I felt so empty

- amba elieff

Maiden, Mother, Crone

There is a weight
to calling you
I feel it
heavy
like lead
and I dread
how the call
will leave me feeling
disconnected
beyond empty
depleted
guilty
longing for a relationship
that doesn't exist
longing for something more
than an obligation

- amba elieff

Maiden, Mother, Crone

I shed his name
like a snake sheds
it's skin
slow and intentional
and ready to be
reborn and grow
New
no attachments to the past
only a future

- amba elieff

Maiden, Mother, Crone

CRONE

Maiden, Mother, Crone

Maiden, Mother, Crone

I own my age
so few women do
I lived every gray hair
each wrinkle
and the crackling of blood vessels and veins like
sponged pottery on my legs
the squishy middle that carried babies
I live in comfortable clothes
the days of fashion
and trying to look cute
or sexy
or fashionable
or appropriate
gone
Inside I have given up believing in fairy tales
and happy endings
and ever afters
I have learned and lived and destroyed convictions
to own my wisdom
my truths - myself...I own all of me

- amba elieff

Maiden, Mother, Crone

Look at your hands
what stories they tell
they are all of you
who have they
held
healed
caressed
hit
loved
How many tears have they dried
hands filled with compassion
hands dry, white embossing the wrinkles
dry skin stretched across knuckles enlarged and achy
veins blue bulging like underground rivers trying to
break free
tendons round and rolling as I shift my fingers
mother's hands, massaging hands, workers hands,
grandma's hands
Look at your hands and take a moment to remember
and reconnect with all of you

- amba elieff

Maiden, Mother, Crone

Maiden, Mother, Crone

Once upon a time I had dreams
they were outlandish
doctorate degrees - not just one
travel – everywhere
I would negotiate world peace
I would discover cures for illness
I would be respected, and my words would be valuable
I would be a famous writer
My thoughts would have worth
I would make a difference in the world
I was young

Then I had simple dreams
to be married
to be a mom - a good mom
to be a wife
have someone who loved me
to be happy
I had children
and got to be a mom
I think a good mom
and then I got the unsettling dreams – not quite nightmares
of divorce
and struggle
and being alone
and then my children gone

Untethered by past dreams
I had new ones
they caressed my mind and soul

Maiden, Mother, Crone

They were dreams for me
to wander and explore and grow and live and find joy
and then one day I was old
and my body and mind could no longer dream

- amba elieff

Maiden, Mother, Crone

In my imagination as I got older
There would be laughter
A full cabin with children scampering
Sleeping on screened in porches
Listening to the whippoorwills
Calling to the owls

Then I stopped and I looked at my imagination
And I thought about the long drive from anywhere my kids scatter to
And I thought about the weather and driving to that cabin
In the woods

Away from everything except trees, rocks, water
And I realized that like the Old Man in the Cave
I would spend many holidays alone
Grandchildren may not find
my screened in porch
the call of the whippoorwills at night
and calling to owls
exciting enough
My children may not have time to travel so far
Time is elusive once you have children

In my imagination as I got older
I would build a cabin in the woods
And it would be small and cozy
And my children can visit
But I am okay if they don't

- amba elieff

Maiden, Mother, Crone

I try to make peace with my face
I look at it in the mirror
I thought I was cute once, even a little pretty
But now past 50 I look at my face missing all of its youth
High cheekbones but no more softness or fullness
Dark brown eyes large and wide
no longer full of wonder and light
Lines like parenthesis that ripple out around my mouth
when I smile
I look at myself and think my face gaunt and hard
Cute and pretty have been replaced with worn and weary
Life is written all over me
I stare at that face in the mirror trying to see beauty

- amba elieff

Maiden, Mother, Crone

Then I honestly counted
How old I am
How many years
I have to remain here
How many years til
I can begin the life I have been waiting for
How long I have waited already
Sunrises and Sunsets
And I add the numbers
I question myself
Should I just stop now?
Will there be anything left of me to enjoy when I get there?

- amba elieff

Maiden, Mother, Crone

When I am gone
do not struggle
trying to find
photos of me throughout a life
that was flawed and frayed

Instead, string together
photos of
my hikes
my flowers
my places
my children
my love
those are far better memories
than my face

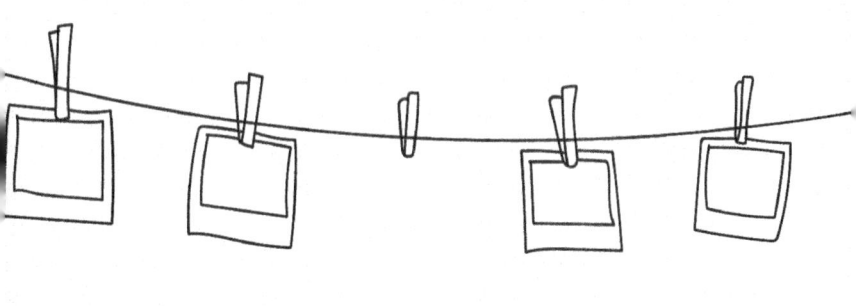

- *amba elieff*

Maiden, Mother, Crone

I didn't procrastinate
this time
I created it
It may be imperfect
It may collect feedback
that makes me cringe inside
makes me want to hide
feel embarrassed
feel wrong
feel inadequate
But I am giving myself a voice
And this time I will honor that voice

- amba elieff

Maiden, Mother, Crone

I thought at 50
when a new half of my life began
a new chapter
All my hard work would provide me security
and time to enjoy life
Life would really begin
I was ready
Life was happening before 50
I was active
When I wasn't tapping on a computer
cleaning house
driving children
I was immersed in nature
I spent days wringing the last drops of sunshine from the skies
soaking up every raindrop for all its wet worth
And delighting in the moon and the stars at night
And then I turned 50 and all that changed
Life became existence
The security I had disappeared
I had to work even harder to barely get by
I no longer notice the sunshine
Rain is just wet
And I am in bed before the moon and stars peak out of the sky
I am on the other side now
Just working and waiting
for everything to come to an end

- amba elieff

It was a yellow stickie on the desk
"You were exposed"
Exposed –
I spent an hour with someone who was sick
They didn't know they were sick yet
In a small room massaging them
Now relying on their facemask and my facemask
And washed hands
Will it be enough to protect me from getting sick
Protect my family from getting sick
At home I am in quarantine
Everyone in the house wears masks
I feel like an outcast
Standing off to the side safely away from everyone
I desperately want to be comforted
I want to be held and told it will be okay
but no one can hold me
I stand and look at my husband with my arms
outstretched like a toddler
Knowing he can't do anything
His eyes go soft
He mouths I love you under his mask
I still work – risk was considered minimal since we all
  wear masks
I touch bodies all day long
But no one touches me
Everything feels empty
I come home and there is the awkwardness of standing
  apart
Of not touching – I lay my head on my husband's back – a
  small comfort
I can't imagine how awful it is for someone in the hospital
For them and for their families

I just got a yellow stickie and believe in being careful – I
    don't think I am sick
Six days to get tested
Three days for a result
living in an empty limbo waiting

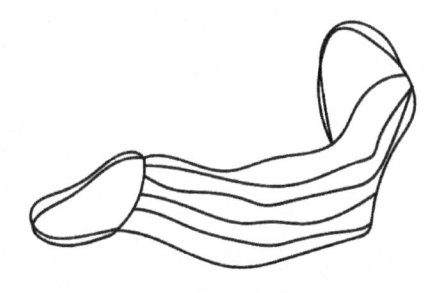

- amba elieff

Maiden, Mother, Crone

Exposed
What does that mean?
Quarantined
Will that keep us safe?
Everyone masks on
Sleeping on the couch
Using the extra bathroom
Staying away from everyone
Not touching anyone
Masks with 6 feet distanced between you and everyone
Sneaking your hand under a blanket to touch your husband's foot
Staring at him across a room
Wishing you could touch him
Be hugged by him
Six days to get tested
Waiting
Three days to get results
Waiting
Because you were exposed

- amba elieff

Maiden, Mother, Crone

Today I realized
you are my life partner
I thought you were my husband
but that is too short
Halfway through life
You are still the boy that caught my eye
and stole my heart
my first kiss
The reason I wouldn't "go" with any other boy
Fourteen
The long gap – my mother created
And much later you were the friend who held my hand
listened to my fears
looked at all my skeletons and broken parts
And chose to love me anyway
And then you became my husband
But really we chose each other a long time ago
At fourteen
And I am sad that we missed those 40 years
But I look at you and still see the boy
My life partner

- amba elieff

Maiden, Mother, Crone

I never imagined at 55 that I would decide that I was old
Decide that at any time I could be done
My children are grown and gone
I work
I write some
I work
I worry
I have no peace
I have not found trust
I am tired of looking
I work
I count down hours to finish days
And days to finish weeks
And weeks to finish months
That make years
By my estimation I need about 10 to get to someplace different
And that is a long time when you are 55
Wanting to finally have some time of your own
Which you have scarcely ever had
So maybe 10 years and maybe done...I keep counting

- amba elieff

Maiden, Mother, Crone

You chose me
never realizing
how fast time
evaporates
into months
and years
And you never realized
the job
My hope
That you would give
me enough good memories
to outnumber
All the years of bad
So I would evaporate one day
surrounded by our memories

- amba elieff

Maiden, Mother, Crone

Life is a struggle
That sometimes is bigger than me
And then I must go to the woods
And look at the trees
That are older - And taller
And have seen so much more than my eyes can hold
And I see that they struggle too
To stretch their roots into the earth
In cracks in rock
Through dirt that is really clay
And they stretch their limbs to the sky - Like hope eternal
Like me
Knowing one day they will die - And feed the earth
I reach out and touch one
Feel the rough bark, scars from peoples' carvings
People have given me scars too not so visible
And I know like the tree
I must go on

- amba elieff

Maiden, Mother, Crone

I wish I were that brave
I was told that when I started buzzing my hair short
I was 40
Brave?
It is hair, it grows, buzzed hair is not brave
Again, I would hear the refrain when I colored my hair purple
I am over 50
I have short buzzed purple hair
Women look at me and say "I wish I were that brave"
Brave is a young girl facing her abuser in court
Speaking her truth in an unwavering voice as he watches on
Brave is another young girl accepting a diagnosis
that means a lifetime of challenges and pain
Living with grace despite it
Brave is a grown woman finding her voice
Being able to speak
Not swallowing the questions and torments
Accepting herself and requiring others to accept her too
Brave is the person living with cancer that has no cure
That stalks her body day and night
Just letting her forget so it can remind her again

Purple hair is not brave
Buzzed hair is not brave
They are audacious in a society that wants us to color within the lines
But then not audacious because my only risk is what you think of me
And I am learning to find my voice, accept myself, and have you accept me too
That is when I am brave...

- amba elieff

Maiden, Mother, Crone

Remind me again
how when you look at me
you see my younger self
The one you barely knew
Remind me how my skin was soft and supple
How my hair dark black shone in the sun
And how my brown eyes sparkled with the light
shining through them
revealing my soul
And slowly I can see myself with my flat belly
And legs firm and fit
Skin kissed by the sun tan and warm
As you gently kiss me
And whisper you will always be young

- amba elieff

Maiden, Mother, Crone

Black silicone band
in the parking lot
blacktop
someone's wedding band
cheaper than gold
more expensive than a cigar band
But not valuable enough
to search for when it slides off a finger
A symbol of promise
once a sacred piece of jewelry
Now an O ring on blacktop
tacky in the afternoon sun

- amba elieff

Maiden, Mother, Crone

Quit comparing yourself
to all of them
any of them
everyone
you aren't perfect
and neither are they
they struggle just like you
they question themselves just like you
they compare themselves to others
just like you
You are as successful, beautiful, intelligent, creative
as you think they are
You just need to start believing it

- amba elieff

Maiden, Mother, Crone

For a moment
imagine
you were wanted
you were never broken
Not the first time
or the second time
the third time
Imagine you
Whole in all your being
See her
Feel her
Be her

- amba elieff

Maiden, Mother, Crone

I woke up
faced with my limitations
A body yesterday
so tired it physically was done
No energy to even open my eyes
Spent
How can I explain being that tired
What are the words
All I can do is reach for the spoons
She told me I get ten spoons a day
There is no adrenaline
to push past ten spoons
When you use them they are gone
You can't get extras
Your body is done
Exhausted, depleted, empty, drained
And now I understand

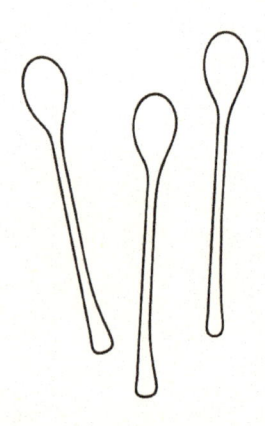

- amba elieff

Maiden, Mother, Crone

Such an old-fashioned desire
but I want to be wooed
just one more time
I want to be wooed by someone who isn't trying to play me
I want someone who is
sincere
because they want me
they love me
they need me
I want to be wooed by someone who is real
not acting
and pretending
to be someone they aren't
to get what they want
not concerned about me
I want to be wooed one more time
so I have one sweet memory
of being chased and desired

- amba elieff

Maiden, Mother, Crone

Some days I am a massage therapist
other days I am a healer
Every day I sacrifice my
hands for you
my fingers and thumbs
Massaging your muscles til they melt
and the knots disappear
Energy floating back and
forth between your body
and mine
healing you
depleting me
over and over
one, two, ten, twenty
bodies
all starved for touch
for relaxation
for healing
And my hands wither away

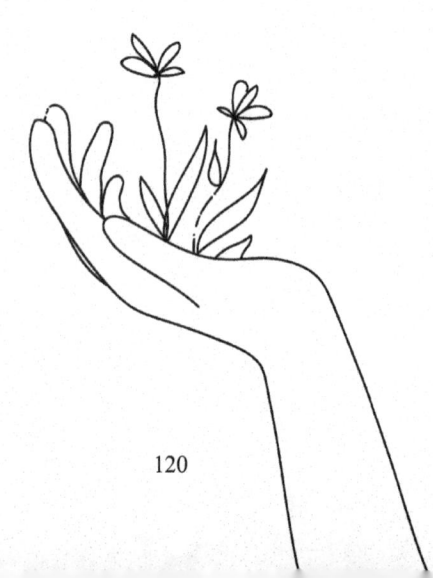

- amba elieff

Maiden, Mother, Crone

And what is the risk
The beginning
One hour in a small massage room
Me with a mask
Client face down without one
We are talking
She tested positive with symptoms the next day
And I wait - And I wonder
And I quarantine
Staying away from everyone in my house
All of us wearing masks
Me sleeping on the couch
And I get tested
And I wait - And I wonder
When I yawn is there more risk?
When I sigh is there more risk?
More particulate matter floating out of the sides of my mask
Should I just stay silent?
Not talk to minimize the risk
Then in the car I am alone and I start singing to the radio
Feels like freedom
I am alone surrounded by risk
And I wait and I wonder – each exhalation what is the risk?

- amba elieff

Maiden, Mother, Crone

I have comfortably entered size 8
a medium
after years of being a 6
struggling to keep my body there
holding it at bay
starving
teasing at times
to be a size 4
tiny
though I never felt thin or small
Now my body gets to relax and just be
an 8
and I will embrace it
and still sometimes eat ice cream
and salads
because I want to
and enjoy them
as an eight

- amba elieff

Maiden, Mother, Crone

I am making myself use the good notebook
to capture my thoughts
the moments
my poetry
I never allowed myself more than a spiral notebook
something that looks
like you could just fill it and throw it in the trash
something school children use
But now I am using the good one
hardbound
with a magnetic clasp
and a fairy decorating the front
sitting on the moon
she could be me
and I am putting my thoughts in it
my creations
because I get to celebrate those thoughts
I get to celebrate my poetry creations
treat them like I am proud of them
and I am worth the good notebook

- amba elieff

Maiden, Mother, Crone

This year on Mother's day
with children flung
around the globe
I realized
I am the end of the line
The last mother
An empty feeling
There are no mothers
or mother-in-laws
or I wished you were my mothers
left to visit
No grandchildren
to create a new batch of mothers
to celebrate
There was nothing to do
no one to celebrate
no dinners
or lunches
gifts
or cards
for a moment it was a lost feeling
being the end
And then a little liberating

- amba elieff

Maiden, Mother, Crone

And 55 stole in
silently
and took her
and no one noticed
or said a word

- amba elieff

Maiden, Mother, Crone

In my mind
I turn around
and look back
from where I now stand
so many paths
never married
later married
different husband
more education
travel
no children
more children
different jobs
different friends
and I wonder
why didn't I see all those paths
why didn't I see all those options
And now I am here
and I look forward
searching for the hidden paths

- amba elieff

Maiden, Mother, Crone

I am in-between old
and alone
and she asked
who are your maidens?
young ones who want advice
that you guide and spend time with
I have none
who are your mothers?
ones who spend time with you
to gain your advice and wisdom
I have none
who are your crones?
to guide you to the next place
the wisdom keepers
the sages
I have none
I am alone
simply me
wandering

- amba elieff

Maiden, Mother, Crone

A shopping spree
my last shopping trip
pairs of shorts
my favorites
worn and in tatters
finally need replaced
near fifteen years old
should have bought more then
but not long after I couldn't find more
and I still can't find more of my favorite shorts
So I found a new favorite
shorts
I bought in duplicates
30 years worth
should last me
so it is my last shopping trip

- amba elieff

Maiden, Mother, Crone

I don't belong here
how many times
have I felt this phrase
and ignored it
not spoken it
knowing I was no longer a part of something
but clinging to it
because I want to belong somewhere
I want to belong
but this time I spoke it
I drew a line
not really belonging anywhere
accepting it
announcing it

I don't belong

- amba elieff

Maiden, Mother, Crone

Maiden, Mother, Crone

The blank page
is my sacred space
it patiently waits
for me to press the pen
into it
and flow my being
onto it
in words
that are my
thoughts, feelings, memories
embodied on that sacred page
a piece of me
I will share with the world

- amba elieff

Maiden, Mother, Crone

Find a moment
when your soul is content
and your body is exhausted
relish in that moment
close your eyes
feel
the peace in your body
content and no longer fighting

- amba elieff

Maiden, Mother, Crone

Losing words
It was subtle
on the tip of my tongue
And then the word was there
Then an esoteric word
trying to find
searching my mind
trying to find a letter
trying to remember what it sounds like
Searching
Thinking
Trying to not think to see if the word would appear
And then I capture it
Provenance
Got it
But then I stand in the kitchen
Telling someone to get the...
And I point at it generally in a basket with other things
Trying to find the word
the thing...
with a cup on the end
scoop
Staring at it
Glancing at the soup on the stove
I reach out and grab it and hand it to them
I close my eyes searching
It finally comes
Ladle
The ladle
And I am scared

- amba elieff

Maiden, Mother, Crone

What will be left to see?
Once upon a time
there were lakes, forests, rivers, mountains
Mother Earth's cathedrals
Spectacular
Breathtaking
the fires
and the heat
land parched by drought
lakes and rivers trickles
charred trees
Burned
land blackened
Images
Still life no fruit
Video
Eerie silence
No trees to catch the wind
No insect's hum
No birds or animals
empty
devoid of life
What we don't burn we topple
Mountains scraped flat for coal
for development
Pictures are all that is left to see

- amba elieff

Maiden, Mother, Crone

I take a step
I move like I am tipsy
foot uncertain where the floor is
searching to see if the floor will come up to meet my foot
or
if my foot will meet the floor
A slight sway
I reach out, hold onto the wall
As my straight lines arc
following the curve of an
invisible rainbow the path of my eyebrow
the bend of a river
and I am floating
flowing
and suddenly
everything is firm again
my step is sure
the earth is stable
and I continue on

- amba elieff

Maiden, Mother, Crone

There is a dark place
I go sometimes
I sit with all my demons
they taunt me
I used to lower my eyes
ashamed of them
afraid of them
ashamed of me
Then one day
in that dark place
I looked at each of them
and called them out by name
And now I don't have to go there anymore

- amba elieff

Maiden, Mother, Crone

The hardest thing about aging
is my body
not the wrinkles
the grey in my hair
the failing eyes
or even the extra width around my waist
It is the surprises
waking up to a body I no longer can trust
A body that at any moment might abandon me to dizziness
unable to walk a straight line
or spring a fever of 100.6
I am not sick
my body is just inflamed and pissed
then my mind joins in and decides to play hide and seek with my vocabulary
And I am trapped in this body

- amba elieff

Maiden, Mother, Crone

We are the daughters
you did not want
the ones you
regretted
tolerated
blamed
ignored
the ones that changed your life
changes that you didn't want
we felt the weight of your baggage
all our lives
until we
allowed ourselves to ask the questions
find the truths
the story – our story
of why you couldn't love us
and then we finally
could love ourselves

- amba elieff

Maiden, Mother, Crone

Daughters
cast off in plain sight
clothed and fed
housed and active
smart and brave
alone
no one sees
how hollow
every gesture
conversation
gift
Daughters
longing to feel
what it is to be wanted

- amba elieff

Maiden, Mother, Crone

The amount of tired in my body
how much can it hold
I ponder this
as my arms and legs start feeling heavy
my eyes struggle to stay open
what was the last thing
the one that put me over the edge
I can't grasp it
only how exhausted
and it feels bottomless
and I must sleep
but when

- amba elieff

Maiden, Mother, Crone

Don't say yes
just because
you believe
no one else will ask

- amba elieff

Maiden, Mother, Crone

The child who gave me hope
Annie
Bright eyes under those long blonde bangs
Animated smiles
comfortable in her skin
As a two-year old should be
After watching
so many
children
glazed eyed at a screen
phone
tablet
too loud
mindless
Annie and her coloring books
a beautiful kaleidoscope
of animation

- amba elieff

Maiden, Mother, Crone

How will I know
when I am full
when I am done
I haven't stopped yet
how much more life
will flow in and out of me
Will I know when it is time to rest

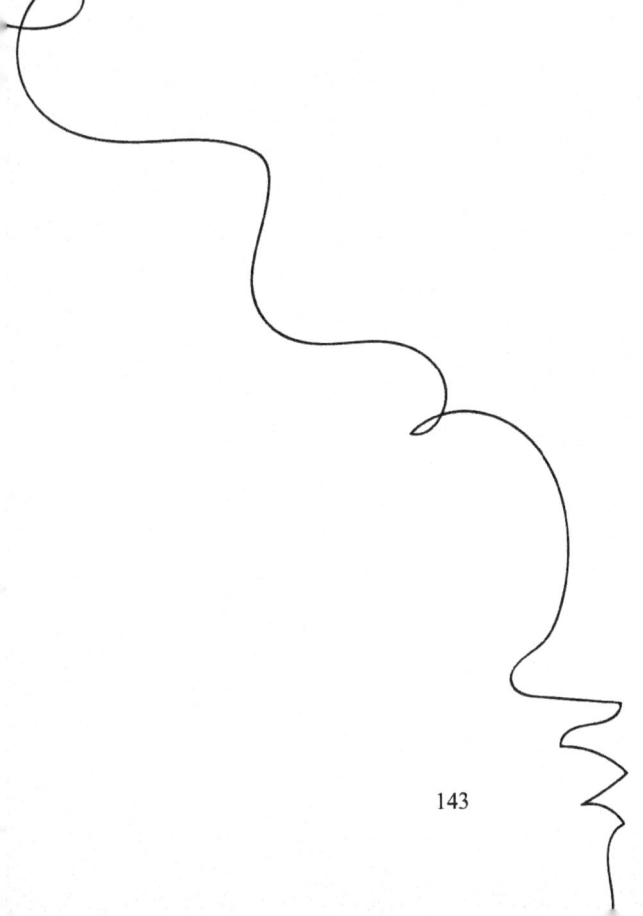

- amba elieff

Maiden, Mother, Crone

This time
when the hours
were cut
so much more
gentle and tender
than being let go
the difference between
small business
and
corporate
I heard the universe
no longer a whisper and nudge
screaming
time to spread your
wings and fly

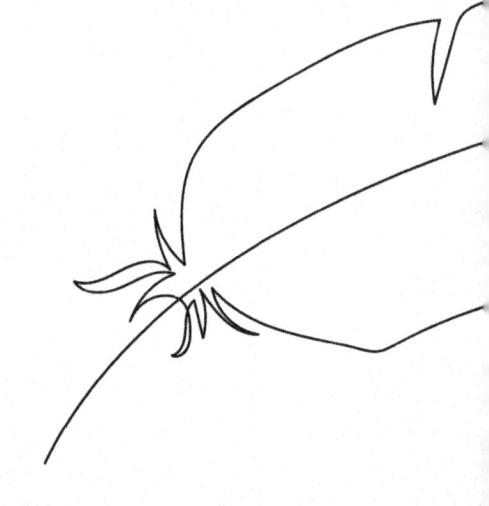

- amba elieff

Maiden, Mother, Crone

A feather
from the quill of a pen
from an angel's wing
from the phoenix rising
Amba

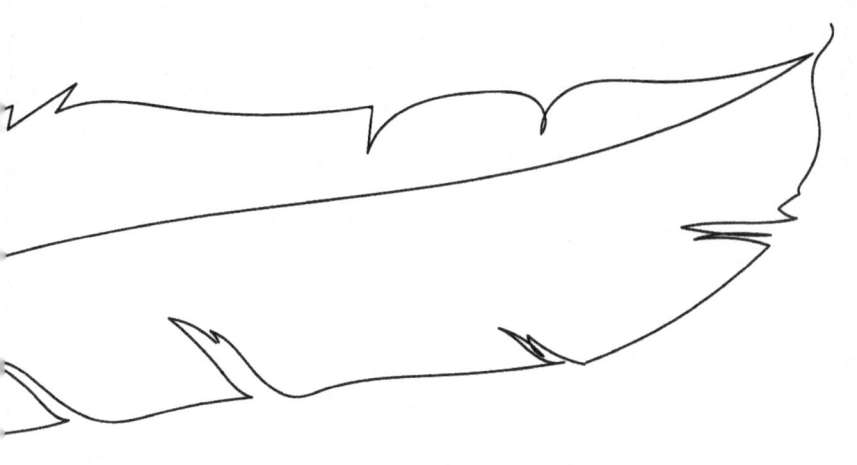

- amba elieff

Maiden, Mother, Crone

I was a grandmother
for a moment
when you were uncertain
before you peed on a stick
and I saw teeny tiny toes
and iddy biddy clothes
and smelled sweet baby smells
and felt soft baby bellies
a touch of excited
and then
you peed
and
the moment passed

- amba elieff

Maiden, Mother, Crone

Maiden, Mother, Crone

You deserve to be chosen
by him
over and over
every day
over and over
for always

- *amba elieff*

Snowflakes
Angels falling from the sky
no two are alike
and they bless us all
and cleanse the soul

- amba elieff

Maiden, Mother, Crone

The landscape of my childhood is gone
Obliterated
Flattened
Demolished
The place where I was born high on the hill is a grassy field
Amongst the rich houses
Once added and scabbed onto wandering like a funhouse maze
Gone

The place where I got my first ice cream cone
A pile of rubble, trucked away filled in with dirt
Across from the Train Depot
Next to a park where children before my time played
Covered over in my time with a gas station
Now gone

The place where I learned the alphabet, made my first friends, learned about the world
With its round kindergarten room, with the fireplace for looks and story time
My first community
My first world
Gone but the handful of bricks I salvaged
Tucked away
Given to close friends who went there too

The place where I fell in love with science and reading and learned I had value
I learned I was smart and witty and would be someone someday
The fence is around it

Maiden, Mother, Crone

They are preparing to tumble down the almost 100 year
    old bricks, granite, slate
That cradled and raised me and many others
There will be a green field here too eventually
And the landscape where I grew up is now flat

The buildings that were my history are gone
They live in my memory with the people I met and loved
I must visit them there sometimes
It reminds me that I came from someplace and grew

- amba elieff

Maiden, Mother, Crone

Maiden, Mother, Crone

Memories now return
yellow gold radioactive signs
in the basement of the middle school
fallout shelter
tornado drills
that were the same
as bomb drills
we didn't know
same basement
head against the wall
crouched down in a ball
butt on cold granite
walls 12 inches thick
schools were solid then
made for 100 years
false security
safe if it is a tornado
destruction
if the bomb
actually came

- amba elieff

Maiden, Mother, Crone

In my mind I look at me
Top to bottom
I am looking for me
The little girl
Who could become anything
The little girl before the world, her mom, society, culture
Defined her
I close my eyes and look at my head
inside my mind
All around my brain full of schooling, living, wisdom
At my brown eyes I so wanted to be blue
At my mouth with the smile that is always awkward
I move my sight to my body
Broad shoulders for a girl
Long arms
Flat chest
She isn't there

Maiden, Mother, Crone

My heart
Beating, rhythm, I look and listen for her
She isn't there
My belly button
An insey – nope
My pelvis and legs
Butt that sticks out
Large thighs and calves
Feet tiny and petite
I don't see her anywhere
Then I hear a whisper
It is from inside my soul
She is there waiting for me
She whispers "Just like who you are..."

- amba elieff

Maiden, Mother, Crone

I like the anonymity
of black and white
the image of a feather
floating
through my life
sharing my life
touching your life
for a moment
with a poem

- amba elieff

Maiden, Mother, Crone

Feet
pictures of my feet
in boots
mostly
places I have been
alone
proof I was there
proof I exist

- *amba elieff*

Maiden, Mother, Crone

I was an obligation
growing up
until I was married
again when I was divorced and single
until I was married again
Now you are an obligation
It is my turn
we are even

- amba elieff

Sometimes I Google
your name
just to see if you
are still alive
certain no one
will tell me
if you die

- amba elieff

Maiden, Mother, Crone

I slide back and forth in time
trying to hold onto a memory
a thought
long enough
to remember the story
catch a moment of feeling
that moment
but they slip away
so quickly
one moment a child
next a grown woman
trying to
what
it is gone

- amba elieff

Learn to say no
or the world will use you up

- amba elieff

Maiden, Mother, Crone

Educated worker bee
working at a steel mill
dangerous
young
a little experience
good looking
travel
national and international
customer sites
never home
schmoozing
personable
never home
perpetuated a marriage
then family
request not to travel
lots of jobs
lots of different groups
problem solver jobs
years here
years there
special projects
shipped overseas to set up sites
spread wisdom
over continents
then aged

Maiden, Mother, Crone

retirement imminent
handful of years left
crap jobs
hard on the body
breathing in filth
sneezing out black
crawling through dirt, grease, grime
clothes and face black like a coal miner
they have used up the education
ready to be done with you

- amba elieff

Maiden, Mother, Crone

A movement starts
with one person
willing
to begin
an uncomfortable
unpopular
conversation
over
and
over
and
over
til another voice
joins in

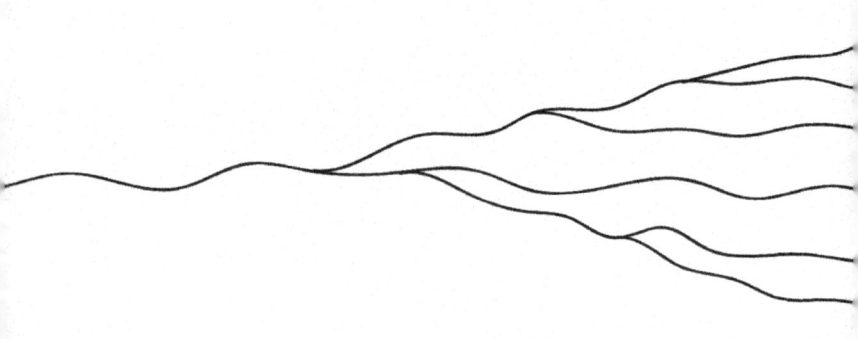

- amba elieff

Maiden, Mother, Crone

The world
opened
another childhood memory
a drawer
in my mind filled
with the fear
and strength
of a ten year old girl
who believed the world
could be safe
believed adults just needed
to listen to the children
and love them
more than they loved hate
and the waking dreams
at night
in bed
of the important adults
who had the bombs
listening to her
a child
reasonably explain
that the children were scared
that we can all get along
that we just need to be friends
and talk
and share
and the scariness of war
can all go away

- amba elieff

Maiden, Mother, Crone

What will be left
when we are gone
what will they find
decorative
water tight boxes
buried underground
treasure inside
what we found precious
metal parts
plates and screws
balls with long stems
what were they for
metal pieces that fit together
like a small rocker
a part for a machine?
sprinkles of rings
some with semi-precious stones
nothing else
merely dust
coating the bottom of the box
creating a soft cushion
for all the metal

- amba elieff

Why do I write poetry?
it is cheaper than doctors
pharmaceuticals
drugs
alcohol
it soothes my soul
speaks my truth
and actually
if you piece
all of the poems together
you will know my story

- amba elieff

PROMPT ME

This is a fun section in each of my volumes of poetry where I share poems that were created and inspired by poetry prompts from online groups on Instagram and other poetry prompt challenges. The hardest thing for me with poetry prompts is following the rules (keeping to word limits) and picking the poem. Every prompt has so many poems hidden inside if you turn the words in your mind. Different viewpoints, different voices, endless possibilities. I hope you enjoy reading these as much as I enjoyed the challenge of writing them.

Maiden, Mother, Crone

Poetry Prompt: I shed words. This was my first poetry prompt submission ever. There was no word limit. There was a time limit, but I don't remember what it was. Ended up with 3 poems. Enjoy.

This first poem is about the place where I wrote all my papers my first year in college.

>In a clearing
>Seven sycamores
>large and old
>wise
>peeling and shedding
>bark
>white, green, brown
>in curls surrounding me
>Leaves larger than my hand
>Growing above secret water
>buried creeks
>Like the secrets in my soul
>this is my writing place
>my sacred space
>where
>I shed words
>on paper
>once a tree
>
>*- amba elieff*

Maiden, Mother, Crone

and I cheated here and tweaked it :)

I shed his name
like a snake sheds
it's skin
slow and intentional
and ready to be
reborn and grow
New
no attachments to the past
only a future

- amba elieff

Maiden, Mother, Crone

I shed words
like a snake sheds its skin
being reborn
words creating emotions
creating feelings
on paper
shedding them
to be reborn
less words
less baggage
new me

- amba elieff

Poetry Prompt: kisses from hell. This challenge had a word limit of 25 and had to be completed in 24 hours. When I first saw the prompt I got so excited that the following poem flowed from my mind onto paper and I loved it. Then I was re-reading the rules and saw the word limit. Ooops. But I really liked this poem. And then as I was putting this section of the book together the last poem emerged from the visions of war.

Maiden, Mother, Crone

Under the stars
She built a fire
nursing it
slowly
like she did their love
when she believed in it
when she thought it was magic
surrounded by piles
pictures, letters, cards, dried flowers, dried sage leaves, clothes, hairbrush
the physical remnants of his cunning, lies and deceit
the fire is now raging
flames licking the air
she tosses in piles of pictures
the acrid smell and green smoke
rises
watching the colors melt
his face now warped
then black and gone
she sprinkles sage on the fire
the cleansing scent
as the last photo burns
Now cards and letters
black paper floating up into the air
Jewelry
rings that were meant as promises
lies and stories - earrings and necklaces
more sage
His hairbrush with the white wisps of hair
now ash
The fire snaps and crackles
talking back

repeating the lies
mocking her
she throws in the clothes, his favorite pillow
every other reminder of him
the flames engulf it
now a part of the fire
The smell of the fire blends
with the sage
She begins to dance
face to the heavens
twirling around the fire
free
arms outstretched
sparks fly
like bursts of fireworks
a hot spark lands
a kiss from hell
on her arm
not fast enough
no water
a blister
that will scar
marked by freedom

- amba elieff

And so I turned the thoughts in my head and here is a different poem with the word limit.

>Under the stars
>the fire raged
>flames lighting the sky
>sparks flying
>creating smaller
>fires
>kisses from hell
>that would burn and scorch
>everything
>
>*- amba elieff*

Maiden, Mother, Crone

And we knew
as the soldiers advanced
bombs and shells exploding
kisses from hell
all around us
keeping
far enough away
to not see our faces
to not see that we look like them
to not see that we are just like them
to not see the simple difference
that we are fighting to stay free

- amba elieff

Poetry Prompt: Worthy, madness, rare. Poem that is 35 words or less using these three words preferably in that order

Following the word count rule:

> In the woods
> she worthy
> the madness and riot
> of flowers
> on the forest floor
> tell her so
> and she
> is a rare blossom
> among them
>
> *- amba elieff*

Maiden, Mother, Crone

But this was my first one and my favorite.

She worthy
of a star in the sky

She madness
like an ice storm - sparkling, shimmering everywhere

She rare
like an eclipse of the sun

She worthy
of much more than me

and

She mine

- amba elieff

Maiden, Mother, Crone

Poetry Prompt: cries of crows, 40 words, in 48 hours. I did not submit this to the poetry prompt challenge. I just liked the prompt and knew I wanted to eventually use it. And then the war began and I was finally ready to write. Hooded crows are actually crows that live in Ukraine. Crows are known to signal by cawing to their flock when danger is near.

> All was silent
> eerie
> heavy silence
> til the cries of hooded crows
> pierced the air
> a warning well before
> the tanks rumbled in
> and the explosions began
> booming, deafening
> cascading shrapnel and cement
> twisted steel
> and glass
> everywhere
> people hidden
> in tunnels and basements
> like moles
> and the crows take flight
> their warning unheard
>
> *- amba elieff*

Maiden, Mother, Crone

ABOUT THE AUTHOR

My name is Amba Elieff and I have been a closet poet my entire life. Writing poetry was my way of making sense of my world and emotions.

While I was writing poetry I was also experiencing life. I survived childhood and went to college. Got married and divorced. Had children. Had other relationships, some I probably shouldn't have. Worked for a "large corporation" most of my life only to have them lay me off at the age of 50 – so I went back to school and became a massage therapist and started over again. But this time starting over I had a wonderful husband who has always known I was a closet poet. And he also told me one day I would write a book. So I have started putting all those years of writing into volumes of poetry, and this is the beginning of my coming out of the closet.

I always imagined being published and now I am. I am Amba and I am a poet.